YORKSHIRE ALPHABET

compiled by

John Hewitt

DALESMAN BOOKS
1976

60p.

**THE DALESMAN PUBLISHING COMPANY LTD.
CLAPHAM (via Lancaster), NORTH YORKSHIRE**

First published 1976

Ⓒ   John Hewitt, 1976

ISBN : O 85206 372 5

Printed in Great Britain by
GEORGE TODD & SON
Marlborough Street, Whitehaven

FOREWORD

YORKSHIRE ALPHABET was first published in 25 weekly instalments in Bradford's evening newspaper, the Telegraph and Argus. No, the alphabet hasn't diminished since your schooldays. I had bravely set myself the task of filling half a page of newsprint with perhaps a dozen or so items and photographs on every letter including the tricky ones of Q, U, X and Z. When I came to X, I had a moment of sheer desperation. Apart from an obscure xylophone player I could find nothing beginning with the noxious letter. I suppose I could have taken the soft option and delved into festive lore under the heading of Xmas. Despite its ancient lineage (even Christopher is shortened to Xopher in some old documents) I have never liked the abbreviation and I decided I wasn't going to start using it now, no matter how great the temptation. So X is missing.

As for the rest of the alphabetical family I found most difficulty with E, J and oddly enough, N. Z, of course presented some problems, but most were solved by a winter visit to Flamingo Park Zoo with a wild north-easter howling round our ears, drowned only by a grim-looking Bengal tiger who eyed us eagerly. Clearly cold weather made him feel hungry.

It was the most common letters of all which gave me sleepless nights. With so many places and people beginning with A, B, D, S and W, what and who should I leave out! I wasted a good deal of time thumbing through books and newspaper cuttings before I could make up my mind. Which is an appropriate cue to thank the small staff of the Telegraph and Argus's excellent newspaper library (one of the finest in the country), several of my colleagues who helped, especially on the sporting, photographic and illustrative side, and the authors of so many books on Yorkshire which I consulted. There are many items, however, which you will not find elsewhere no matter how assiduously you seek, being the result of personal interviews with Yorkshire people. Because the alphabet was written for a Bradford newspaper, it is inevitable that it should be rooted in the West Yorkshire area. But in compiling this book I have widened its scope to include, in particular, Wensleydale, Swaledale and the moors and coastline around Whitby and Scarborough for which I have a deep affection.

The whole affair is a personal anthology of facts, anecdotes, unusual snippets of information, customs and biographies, a patchwork of

Yorkshire, past and present, punctuated with a little humour. I apologise in advance if your favourite hero, heroine or celebrated town is absent from these pages. I can only say that I have not tried to make the alphabet completely comprehensive. Yorkshire is so large and variagated, so chock-a-block with characters and character, that it would be impossible in any publication short of a 21-volume encyclopaedia.

— John Hewitt

The cover design by J. J. Thomlinson shows: Coal mining in South Yorkshire; Hardraw Force; Ilkley Moor; Robin Hood's Bay; and Skipton Castle.

The publishers gratefully acknowledge the loan of illustrations and blocks by the Telegraph & Argus, Bradford. All uncredited illustrations in the text are from this source.

ILLUSTRATIONS

A Yorkshire Alphabet in Pictures

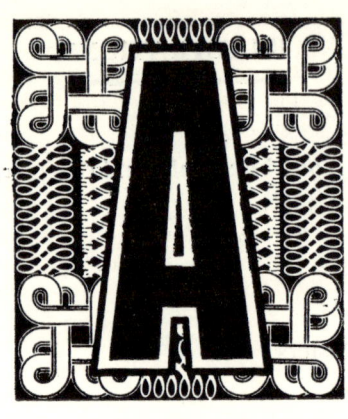

ALUM : Like mountains of the moon, the great mounds of spoil from the old alum works on the East Coast are an eerie spectacle on their deep shelf half way up the cliffside running from Saltburn to ten miles south of Whitby. Once an Italian monopoly, alum production was brought to Yorkshire in the late 16th century by Sir Thomas Chaloner of Guisborough who was cursed by the Pope for his pains. Alum was mined on the East Yorkshire cliffs from the beginning of the 17th century and in the heyday of the late 19th century the sight must have been an awe-inspiring one, especially as dusk was falling. To calcinate the alum, miniature "volcanoes" were built, some of them 90-100 feet high, and fired with furze, brushwood and coal. It often took eight to nine months for a "volcano" to be built and another three months for it to burn. It was a wasteful process with 120-130 tons of mined material being needed to produce one ton of alum. Nearer the sea, shallow pits, nearly 50 feet long and linked one to another, were sunk. Here the liquid alum was left to soak. The final process of evaporation took place in long, dark and, one imagines, noisome sheds. The alum was led into large butts to cool and crystalise. The alum has long since been worked out, but the huge heaps remain, gaunt reminders of a forgotten industry.

ANGLING : Britain's number one participation sport with 2.7 million adherents. It has always been extremely popular in the industrial areas of West Yorkshire. Main interest centres on the wide rivers tumbling down the Dales towards the Vale of York — the Swale, Ure, Nidd, Wharfe, Ouse and Derwent which can be fished on day tickets but are mostly controlled by the big angling associations from Bradford, Leeds and York. Predominant species are trout (in the upper reaches), chub and barbel. In 1974 anglers paid £8,000 for $12\frac{1}{2}$ tons of Dutch roach in a desperate bid to re-establish their favourite species which almost disappeared in the 1960s.

HERBERT HENRY ASQUITH : A Yorkshireman from Church Street, Morley, who won a place in history despite modest beginnings. His father and grandfather were Morley woolmen but it is doubtful whether they visualised that the young Asquith would one day become Prime Minister and later Earl of Oxford and Asquith. He lacked the quality of charisma, but as a speaker he was noted for his clarity, brevity and weight. It was said he "drove a Roman road through every subject." But he was man of the heart as well as the head. He went to the Bar at 24, married the following year despite his slender means, and three years later managed to scrape up £300. He spent almost all of it at one fell swoop — on a diamond necklace for his wife.

AYSGARTH : Apart from its beautiful Falls on the River Ure and its museum of horse-drawn vehicles at the old corn mill, the Wensleydale village is famous in a lesser way for Mij, the domino playing dog which was once owned by the warden at the Aysgarth Youth Hostel. **(See photograph on page 17.)**

BLACK DYKE : Yorkshire wouldn't be the same without its brass bands and the most famous of them all is Queensbury's Black Dyke, which first took the national Open championship in 1860 and recently won it for the 20th time. Forerunner of the band was a small reed and brass band formed at Queensbury (then known as Queen's Head) the year after Waterloo. The horn player was a certain John Foster, who later built up his mohair and alpaca business and became known locally as "Old Foster The Money Man." When the little village band fell upon hard times John Foster and his brother William took it over as the mill's official brass band — and set it on the road to greatness.

BOOZE : Beer has always been appreciated by Yorkshiremen. They tend to take their drinking seriously, endlessly discussing the merits of one brew against another. In the old days many publicans, who in country districts were often farmers as well, ran their own brew-houses on the premises. But the great brewing town of Yorkshire is Tadcaster, where they have been brewing ale since the Middle Ages. Booze (the village, not the drink) can be found in Arkengarthdale.

BRIMHAM ROCKS: On the windy moorland near Pateley Bridge lies Britain's most peculiar collection of rocks, soft boulders carved like sea-caves by the action of wind in desert conditions. Around 60,000 visitors a year marvel at the spectacular and grotesque forms, which often resemble animals. Since the National Trust acquired Brimham Rocks, it has renovated the hunting lodge, installed a warden, and laid out new (and controversial) car parks. With the wind and all those nooks and crannies, litter is a big problem and the warden is persistently urging visitors to take their litter home with them.

BRONTE SISTERS: This strange, lonely, short-lived and vastly talented trio has brought to the steeply rising town of Haworth a fame

The Brontë Sisters and Parsonage, Haworth.

8

which it both welcomes and dislikes. Over the past ten years, particularly, the literary pilgrimage has swollen to a flood. Some 250,000 visitors a year toil up the winding hill to the Bronte Parsonage Museum, owned by the Bronte Society, on the edge of the inhospitable moors. A section of the museum is kept as it was in the Brontes' day, but the remainder houses a huge range of historical documents and paintings about the family, a display which is changed at least twice a year. One of its recent acquisitions is so valuable that only photographs can be put on show. It is a £4,000 miniature book, entitled *The Evening Walk* which Charlotte Bronte wrote out in miniscule-longhand at the age of eleven in 1830.

The popularity of Haworth blurs the fact that the Brontes have several other connections in other parts of West Yorkshire. The Rev. Patrick Bronte met and married Maria Branwell while he was minister of the parish of Hartshead-cum-Clifton and in 1815 he moved to a curacy at Thornton, where Charlotte, Branwell, Emily and Anne were born. Opened in 1973 at Gomersal is the Red House Museum. Charlotte Bronte was a close friend of Mary Taylor, who lived at Red House, and they went to school together at Mirfield. The house, which masquerades under the name of "Briarmains," features in her book *Shirley.*

C is a harsh letter, reminiscent of the clints on limestone uplands and the carrion crows which prey on new-born lambs. It is suggestive of ancientry, pre-historic cup and ring boulders, the Wapentake of Craven, clapper bridges — those single slabs crossed by packhorse ponies — the skeletal Cowthorpe Oak near Wetherby said to be 1,000 years old, and the ravages of the Civil War.

CASTLE HOWARD : While being used as a girls' school during the war, Castle Howard, near Malton, the first great work of architect Sir John Vanbrugh, narrowly escaped complete destruction. A fire which began in a cupboard in the dining room in 1940 spread rapidly, severely damaging the dome and several state rooms and ruining the painting *The Fall of Phaeton*. Castle Howard survived, however, to become one of Yorkshire's leading tourist attractions. Although it was begun in 1702, Vanburgh had not completed it by his death in 1726. **(See photograph on page 17.)**

THOMAS CHIPPENDALE: It wasn't until a document turned up in 1912 that Otley people were sure the famous cabinet maker had been born in the town. Apart from the fact of his baptism in 1718 little is known of his early life. He apparently worked with his father, Otley joiner John Chippendale, until his work was noticed by the Earl of Harewood. Through this illustrious patronage he was sent to London and apprenticed to a firm of cabinet makers. He set up on his own in Conduit Court, Long Acre, in 1749. Now his furniture is among the most sought after in the world.

CHOIRS: Along with brass bands, choirs are a Yorkshire musical speciality. The county has the oldest choral societies in the country — Halifax and Bradford Old Choral are both over 150 years old — and the famous Leeds Music Festival, inaugurated in 1858 and still the major showpiece for Yorkshire choral singing.

COAL: Yorkshire's prosperity is built upon coal. But until recently it was firmly believed that the rich South Yorkshire coalfield stopped short of Selby. But borings have revealed one of the richest coal strikes in Europe, 1,000 million tons of high quality coal which stretches across 60 square miles from Selby, up and beyond the historic walls of York. The latest methods are being used to extract the coal, and great care will be taken not to damage the beauty of the low-lying meadows.

CAPTAIN JAMES COOK: Acknowledged as one of the greatest navigator-scientists of all time. In three remarkable voyages — the first in the converted collier *The Endeavour* — he shattered the myth of a vast southern continent, landed at Botany Bay, charted eastern Australia and many of the Pacific islands, proved that New Zealand was in fact two islands and incidentally preserved his crew from the dreaded disease of scurvy. Yet this determined and resolute man was born in the most humble circumstances, the son of a day labourer in the village of Marton-in-Cleveland. Fortunately for him his father became foreman on a Great Ayton farm and the owner sent young James to school. At 17 he was apprenticed to a grocer and haberdasher at Staithes and there the sea entered his veins. He transferred his

10

apprenticeship to John Walker, the Whitby Quaker ship-owner. He went to sea during the summer while in the winter he studied hard at mathematics and navigation. It was said that it was on the treacherous seas of the East Coast that he learnt the tricks of the navigating trade which led him to Australia and beyond.

CURLEWS: If Yorkshire has a bird which it could call its own, it must be the curlew, with its curved beak and long and lonely cry, inhabitant not only of the high moors but increasingly the quiet fields in the Dales. Farmers reckon it is a bad weather sign when the curlew is heard during the night. It means, they say, that rain is due.

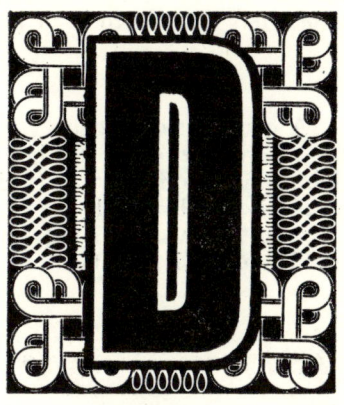

D has about it the open air: the slow meandering of the Derwent which though it rises five miles from Ravenscar on the East Coast flows inland until it reaches the Ouse; and the quick bobbing movements of the dipper, or the Bessie Dooker as countrymen name this bird of rivers and waterfalls. It stands for daffodils, nowhere more famous than the wild ones at Farndale; and drovers who shepherded great herds of cattle and sometimes geese, wearing makeshift "shoes" to save their webbed feet, down from Scotland through the Dales to the Midlands and South. Even the dyeing trade began by extracting colours from flowers and other plants. Now it is a highly sophisticated business in West Yorkshire where there are hundreds of dyeing firms, making dyes not only for wools but a vast variety of man-made fibres.

DALES WAY: For those walkers seeking a less demanding and more low-level route than the Pennine Way, the Ramblers' Association in 1968 pioneered the Dales Way, a 73-mile continuous walk from Ilkley to Bowness on the shores of Windermere. Although not yet officially recognised as a long distance footpath route, it is being used by an increasing number of walkers each year. As far as is known the record for completing the route is 3¼ days.

DELIUS : The Yorkshire moors had more attraction than the dingy black Bradford warehouse for Frederick Delius, destined to become one of the world's finest composers. Although he was destined for the wool trade, he showed little interest in it and at 22 went to Florida to grow oranges! His keen interest in music led him to devote himself to full time writing and after studies in Leipzig and a taste of "gay Paree" he eventually settled in Grez-sur-Loing near Fontainebleau, where blind and in failing health he produced his undoubted masterpieces with the aid of another Yorkshireman, the young Eric Fenby, who acted as his ammenuensis. His music today is still an acquired taste for many, but of late has established itself in the hearts of many music lovers.

DOCK PUDDING : A centuries-old delicacy in the Calder Valley, one of the few places where the sweet tasting dock grows. When the World Dock Pudding championship was held at Hebden Bridge it was won by housewife Berry Horsfall, who defied the wiseacres and made it without the nettles, which experts say are necessary for top class dock pudding. To make it you need a bagful of the special

The Dropping Well, Knaresborough
(J. J. Thomlinson)

sweet docks — and the small leaves too. The ordinary cow dock just tastes horrid. You must carefully cut up the leaves and boil them with onions and seasoning until they are soft and tender. When most of the water has evaporated stir in enough oatmeal to bind the docks together. Delicious, so Calder Valley folk say.

DROPPING WELL : At Knaresborough is one of Yorkshire's great curiosities and one which is visited by tens of thousands of people every year. It is often referred to as a petrifying well, but in fact the variety of objects hung there are not really turned to stone. They are coated with calcium which is carried by a rivulet falling over the cliff into the Nidd. John Leland who visited Knaresborough in 1540 described it thus : ". . . a Welle of wonderful nature, caullid Droping Welle. For out of the great Rokks by it distillith water continually into it. This water is so cauld and of such a nature that what thing so ever . . . ye caste in, or growith about the Rokke and is touched of this water growith into stone."

EASBY ABBEY : So generous were the monks of the 12th century Easby Abbey that it was almost their undoing. Most poor people who called at the Abbey were treated to food and drink and many doles, some established by the Scrope family of Castle Bolton, provided for their relief. Every day, for instance, from All Souls' Day to the Feast of the Circumcision they gave a flagon of ale, a loaf of bread and a piece of flesh to one pauper, costing £1 6s 8d a year. And on St. Agatha's Day they spent £4 on corn and fish for all needy people in the area, and £4 for alms to poor people who on that and two succeeding days came to Communion. They spent so much on alms-giving that at the Dissolution the Abbey's total revenue came to little over £100.

EASTER EGGS: In several pockets of hilly West Yorkshire the custom still continues of Pace or Pasche Egging which is a matter of rolling decorated hard boiled eggs down a slope until they break. A favourite way of colouring them is to wrap the egg in onion skins, bound on with an elastic band and to boil in water coloured with cochineal.

Cracking an egg the hard way

EBORACUM: Ancient capital of Yorkshire, the walled city of York was known to the Romans as Eboracum. A great legionary fortress, it became under Emperor Severus the capital of Northern (or Lower) Britain—the second most important city in the land. It was while the Romans were fighting their ruthless war against the Brigantes that Eboracum first became a Roman fortress, the permanent home of the Ninth Legion from A.D. 71. It was chosen, not because it was easily defensible, but because it was central, an ideal jumping off place for the attacking legions. Some 1800 years later the same sort of thinking made York the pivot of the Northern railway network. Eboracum was closely connected with three Roman Emperors. It was there that the veteran warrior, Emperor Severus, died in 211 worn out by his campaigns against the Picts. Nearly a century later Eboracum was to have the magnificent honour of proclaiming a new Emperor who was to become one of the great names of Imperial history. Constantius, who held the title of Caesar or junior Emperor, had brought many reforms and prosperity to Britain. When he died in Eboracum in 306 Constantine, his illegitimate son by Helena, a British woman of lowly birth, claimed the title of Caesar. He defeated his rivals and seven months later became sole Emperor, the illustrious Constantine the Great, the first Christian Emperor.

ESK : The romantic story of how the River Esk, which runs through the North Yorkshire moors to Whitby, acquired a bridge is still re-told in the area. It is said that Thomas Ferres who came to Egton as a tramp arranged to meet his girl friend on the banks of the Esk. Unfortunately on the night of the tryst the Esk was swollen with floodwater and he was unable to cross. He pledged that when he was a wealthy man he would build a bridge so that no other lovers would be similarly frustrated. Other killjoys rather spoil the story by insisting the reason Ferres made the pledge was that he slipped while crossing the stepping stones and was nearly drowned in the flooded river. Whatever the reason the bridge at Glaisdale was built in 1621 and bears the initials of Ferres, who did become a wealthy man and Mayor of Hull. The bridge is known either as "Beggar's Bridge" or "Lover's Bridge" depending which version of the story you prefer.

FAIRIES : After half a century the curious case of the Cottingley Fairies remains an enigma. Sir Arthur Conan Doyle, inventor of Sherlock Holmes and one of Spiritualism's most influential advocates, brought the matter into the open with an article in the *Strand Magazine* in 1920. As they played beside Cottingley Beck at Bingley, 16-year-old Elsie Wright, of Lynwood Terrace, Cottingley, and her cousin, Frances Ealing (10), of Scarborough, took photographs with Mr. Wright's quarter plate camera of fairies — diminutive creatures with transparent wings, which, with hindsight, have a very "dated" look. Several experts, however, declared them to be single exposures.

Sir Arthur was convinced and mused on the details of life in the fairy kingdom. But other photographers were sceptical especially when it was revealed that Elsie, described as "a dreamy girl at school", worked in a Christmas card factory and had carried out some drawings for a jeweller. Tracked down and interviewed in recent years the two women have stoutly maintained no fraud was involved but, irritatingly, have refused to be drawn into detailed questioning. Were the photographs of genuine fairies, impressions of mental images, or is the answer really fraud? After all these years the tantalising mystery remains. **(See photograph on page 18.)**

GUY FAWKES : Being burned in effigy once a year is hardly a fit fate for a Yorkshireman, especially one who displayed the courage of Guy (or Guido) Fawkes. Discovered on November 4, 1605, guarding 36 barrels of gunpowder in the cellars at the House of Lords, this York-born soldier of fortune was hauled into James I's bedchamber and cross-examined. He was then put to the "gentler tortures" to reveal the names of his accomplices, but it was not until he underwent the most severe tortures, leaving him a broken man, that he confessed.

It is suggested by modern historians that Fawkes was the victim of a cruel charade, that the King, through his influential councillor Robert Cecil, knew of the Gunpowder Plot well in advance and was using it as an excuse to bring further pressure to bear on England's Catholics. Ironically, Guy Fawkes was born a Protestant, the son of lawyer Edward Fawkes, one of the Fawkes of Farnley Hall. But when his father died, his mother remarried a Roman Catholic, Denis Bainbridge, and the family moved to Scotton Old Hall and later Percy Hall near Scotton. Caught up in the social life of the Hall and becoming acquainted with some of the leading Catholics of the day it was hardly surprising that the young Guy Fawkes should become an enthusiast for the faith. It led him to join the Spanish Army in the Low Countries, to become an authority on explosives and finally to pay the ultimate price. In the end, however, he cheated the executioner. Condemned to be half-hanged, drawn and quartered, he tottered up the scaffold and then leapt, breaking his neck as he fell.

FISH : An odd custom carried out by fishermen on the Yorkshire coast was that of "paying for the fish." As the nets were being let down, a cork would be slit open and a coin, preferably a silver one, inserted. Without the payment, the fishermen could not expect success. Fish caught off Flamborough Head appear to have been unusually omniverous. Articles found inside cod in the late 19th century included a wooden doll, a pair of unbroken spectacles and a coral necklace. One codfish obviously lived a dangerous life. Inside it were found 59 hooks. The sixtieth caught it!

Aysgarth Falls, which some writers have regarded as surpassing the
cataracts of the Nile   (F. Leonard Jackson)

Castle Howard on fire, when it was being used as a school in 1940

Fairies at Cottingley, one of a series of controversial photographs taken
in 1917 by Elsie Wright

The Leeds-Liverpool Canal and the famous Five Rise Locks at Bingley
(Clifford Robinson)

Gaping Ghyll Main Chamber (J. O. Myers)

19

Mining in the Dales is recalled by this hexagonal powder house at Langthwaite, Arkengarthdale, in which gunpowder for the lead mines was stored (Geoffrey N. Wright)

Quarry Hill Flats, Leeds, built to house 938 families (J. Eccles)

FIVE RISE LOCKS : Just over 200 years old Bingley's Five Rise Locks on the Leeds-Liverpool Canal is recognised as one of the "Wonders of the Canal World." A rise of two locks is a common thing on Britain's canals, but five locks which are arranged so that the top gate of one lock also forms the bottom gate of the next with no clear water between is unique. The Five Rise gives a total lift of 59ft. 2 inches.

G is for the grim, grotesque and gigantic, both in humanity and in nature.

GAPING GHYLL : Most awesome of all Yorkshire's potholes is Gaping Ghyll on the slopes of Ingleborough, a 360ft. sheer drop into a massive cavern leading to a cave system which is still yielding new discoveries. Nowadays both Bradford and Craven Pothole Clubs hold club "meets" there when they lower visitors on a bosun's chair. But the first man to descend, French pioneer potholer Monsieur E. A. Martel, used a rope, his bare hands and some candles. "It was," he recalled "rather uncomfortable when swinging in mid-air with the water dropping over me from above". **(See photograph on page 19.)**

GIANT HOGWEED : A particularly nasty plant it resembles a 10ft. - 15ft. high version of cow parsley. A native of the Caucasians, it escaped from Kew Gardens 63 years ago and is now common on waste land near Keighley, Shipley and Bingley. Its sap can cause burning and discoloration of the skin which can last up to six years. Best give it a wide berth.

GIANTS: A genuine flesh and blood giant was a man named Bradley who was born in Market Weighton in 1787. He was seven foot seven inches tall and his shoes were 15 inches long. After exhibiting himself in London and various other parts of the country, he died in 1811 and was buried in a coffin measuring nine feet by three feet. More pathetic was the "Gigantic Child" Isaac Butterfield born at Keighley in 1781. When 20 months old he was three feet tall and weighed nearly eight stones. He too was put on show but did not live to enjoy his "fame." He died before his second birthday.

GIBBET: Last used in 1650 the Halifax Gibbet (or at least a replica of it made by the local museum) has re-appeared on its original site in Gibbet Street, Halifax. Invented in the 13th century it was a gory guillotine, more properly termed the Halifax Machine. The blunt blade embedded in a 4ft. 6in. block of wood severed the victim's head by its sheer weight. It is estimated that 80 criminals ended their lives on this unique gibbet. As one rhymster put it :

"At Halifax the law so sharp doth deal,
That whoso more than 13 pence doth steal
They have a gyn that wondrous quick and well
Sends thieves all headless to heaven or hell."

GREAT YORKSHIRE SHOW: The highlight of the farming year, the massive three-day Show on its permanent 84-acre site at Harrogate, now attracts well over 100,000 visitors a year. It all began in 1837 with an influential meeting at the Black Swan Hotel, York, chaired by Earl Spencer, former Chancellor of the Exchequer, which founded the Yorkshire Agricultural Society — and launched it with a "whip-round" totalling £435. Right from the start, the Society was forward-looking, offering prizes for the invention and improvement of agricultural implements. At the first show — held in a six-acre barrack yard at York in 1838 — there were 105 horses, 68 cattle, 90 sheep and 38 pigs. For many years the Show venue moved around the county but is now well established on its permanent site at Harrogate.

HARDRAW FORCE: It is difficult to believe that the beautiful and dramatic waterfall which pours over Wensleydale's Hardraw Scar was once shattered and distorted almost out of recognition. It happened in the great flood of 1899 when rainwater sluiced down from the heights of Great Shunner Fell. Thwaite and Muker in Swaledale were badly damaged, and in the village of Hardraw gravestones were ripped from the ground, furniture floated from houses and a tree smashed down on the Green Dragon Inn at the entrance to Hardraw Force. Worse, their cherished tourist attraction, the fall itself was no more. The lip of rock over which the stream pours in a single unhindered fall was gone. The water merely trickled in dribbles down the mound of mud and shale. Bridges had been swept away and surrounding grass bankings had been undermined. Lord Wharncliffe, who owned the land, must have been desolated, though he showed no signs of it. He simply told his estate manager to "Put it all back." So he did, remodelling the crucial lip of rock in such a way that it looked completely natural, and tidying up the ravages in the valley. It was a triumph of landscape renovation.

HARROGATE FESTIVAL: With its reputation now firmly established, the Harrogate Festival was the first in the country to combine the arts and sciences on an equal footing. Now the science side has dwindled but the other arts have shone brighter, with special emphasis on up and coming musicians.

GEORGE HUDSON: Life for George Hudson, "The Railway King," had its ups and downs with a vengeance. Modestly born, the son of a York draper, in 1800, he inherited around £30,000, and seeing the potential of the new-fangled Iron Horse, invested it in railways.

A bold entrepreneur, he determined to make York the centre of the railway system and it is through his business acumen that all lines lead to York. Three times he was Lord Mayor of the city, but fate had a bitter pill in store for him. He had carried out deals without consulting his board of directors and falsified the accounts into the bargain. At last he was found out and he died ruined and disgraced. British Rail have now made some amends. They have named their York Eastern Region headquarters Hudson House.

George Hudson at the time of his downfall in 1849, as depicted by the famous Leech cartoon in "Punch"

SIR LEONARD HUTTON: Yorkshire and England's greatest batsman, the man who made his home town of Pudsey famous throughout the cricketing world, accomplished his magnificent feats despite a war injury which made his left arm two inches shorter than his right. During his years as England's first professional captain, the team was top of the world. He captained England in 23 Tests against every country in the world apart from South Africa and never lost a series. Most important he regained the Ashes and then kept them in the Australian tour of 1953-54. His record tells his story: The world's highest Test score of 364 against Australia at The Oval in 1938 scored in 13 hours 20 minutes; more than 40,000 runs in first class cricket (only bettered by nine other players) and 6,971 runs in Tests, giving a Test match average of 56.67.

ILKLEY MOOR : Known throughout the world, Ilkley Moor is no longer the same place that our grandparents remembered. In the last 70 years it has undergone huge changes — and not all can be laid at the door of day-trippers. Plans are afoot to repair the damage to paths worn down by visitors, especially during the moor's great popularity before 1939. But it is impossible to reverse the changes wrought by nature and the sheep.

Less than a century ago Ilkley Moor was almost totally heather-covered with a couple of large areas of cotton-grass bog with grass and heath on the lower slopes. There was also a great deal of birch scrub which has completely disappeared. Now bracken swamps the hillsides up to 1,000ft. and crowberry has spread alarmingly until it is found almost all over the moor. It is the dominant species in many places. Wharfedale Naturalists' Society which has been surveying the moor in detail since 1959 (with the help at times of aerial photography), places the blame squarely on the sheep. Most of the damage was done between 1914 and 1945 when the flocks of sheep on the moor were at their height. Sheep eat most things, bilberry, young shoots of cotton-grass and heather, which they sometimes pull up by the roots. But crowberry they will not touch. So crowberry has taken over, being helped by the fact that the moor is drying out, and by the accidental fires which leave bare burnt areas for the crowberry to colonise. In recent years, however, sheep grazing has been reduced and the heather is beginning to stage a comeback. Oddly it has been found that the Ilkley Moor sheep nibble the bracken, which is not normally part of a sheep's diet and in fact can sometimes prove poisonous. It appears they tackle dying bracken which is subject to some kind of degeneration particularly noticeable near the 1,000ft. limit. The bracken's troubles leave the door ajar for the ubiquitous crowberry and there are signs that the take-over of the bracken areas in some places is already well advanced.

Of course, Ilkley Moor has been trodden for thousands of years, its inhabitants leaving a selection of worked flints and clients. Bronze

Ilkley Moor and its well-known Cow and Calf Rocks
(A. P. Waterhouse)

Age man came here 3,500 years ago, possibly from Scandinavia and left us the puzzle of the cup and ring stones, more than 100 of them hidden by the heather dotted all over Rombalds Moor. Found in many other countries including America, they were laboriously chipped out of the boulders, usually in a series of concentric circles with a gutter-channel running through them. The most famous of the varied rock markings is the Swastika Stone above Hebers Ghyll, undoubtedly a religious or magical symbol. But what exactly did the cup and ring stones mean and why are they clustered together on the high ground? The mystery still awaits solution.

Mystery also surrounds the Yorkshire anthem itself *On Ilkla' Moor Baht 'At.* It was first published in 1916 to the hymn tune Cranbrook composed by Thomas Clark of Canterbury but had been known and sung for 40 to 50 years before that. No one knows who wrote the words, though it was claimed by several moorland areas including Emley Moor, Ovenden Flat, and even "At Luddendenfoot baht booit." Keighley people used to say it was originally "Hawkcliffe Wood baht 'At" and was written by a Sutton man named Fenegan.

INN SIGNS: Several inns are noted for their signs. The *World's End* inn at Knaresborough showed a coach crashing through the bridge — a reminder of Mother Shipton's prophecy that when the bridge fell three times the world would come to an end. The *Hermit Inn* at

Burley Woodhead, near Ilkley, pictures the Hermit of Rombalds Moor, Job Senior, who lived on the edge of the moor. In remorse for his wife's death, which he believed he had caused, he lived in a kind of dog-kennel on the edge of the moors, eating potatoes roasted on a peat fire.

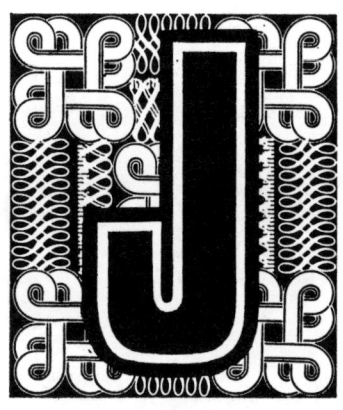

JET : The black semi-precious stone which was used for ornaments in early Bronze Age times is once again coming into fashion. Its value has shot up in the last three or four years and the few remaining jet turners in the Whitby area are inundated with orders. Its increasing popularity is bringing rich pickings for the beachcombers who scour the Whitby sands for pebbles of "Black Amber" as it is called locally — the fossilised resin of ancient monkey puzzle trees which grew in this part of Britain several million years ago. But for the craftsmen only flawless pieces of jet will do. The big jet craze came in the mid-19th century when Queen Victoria chose it for State mourning following the death of Prince Albert. After that no fashionable woman would be seen without buttons, brooches or a crucifix made from Whitby jet. The first mines were opened up at Sandsend and later at Overdale and Loop Wyke and the east side of Runswick Bay. As demand grew they moved inland along the hillside from Guisborough to Roseberry Topping. The north and north-west slopes of the Cleveland Hills are still pockmarked by long abandoned mine shafts. The industry reached its peak in 1873 when it turned over more than £90,000 a year with 1,500 people employed. About 200 of them were miners who hunted the cliffs and hills for new seams of jet to keep the Whitby workshops busy. But the fashion faded and in a remarkably swift time the entire jet industry collapsed.

JOWETT CARS : Bradford might be the centre of Britain's motor car industry if the two Jowett brothers, Ben and Willie, had put quantity before quality. But like true Yorkshiremen they were determined to do things their way. Instead of expanding their firm Jowett Cars Ltd. after the 1914-18 war, they kept production down to 25 cars a week and accepted not a penny of outside money until 1935, ensuring that every vehicle they produced was individually made. Today proud owners of Jowett cars swear by their qualities of road holding, comfort and quality. There is even a Jowett Car Club composed of enthusiastic owners from all over the country.

The first Jowett car

It was Ben Jowett, who died in 1963, aged 86, who launched the business in a small cycle shop in Church Street, Bradford, in 1901. Shortly afterwards he was joined by his younger brother Willie Jowett, who died in 1955 at the age of 74. It was only after moving to Grosvenor Road, Bradford, that they decided to build their first car. Made in 1906 it weighed six hundredweight, was fitted with a two-cylinder horizontally opposed water-cooled engine and kept motoring costs down to around a penny a mile. But they were so busy making Scott-Jowett motor cycles that it was several years before they could be bothered to put the car into full production. Their best cheap-to-run family car was the Long Saloon which appeared in 1928 in days when petrol was 1s a gallon. It was a nippy runabout which clocked up to 47 miles per gallon and gave the working man a chance of owning a car. "It used to amuse me to overtake and leave standing much larger cars on hills," chuckled one happy owner. "For the Jowett was born and bred as a hill climber."

During the 1939-45 War, Jowett's eccentric methods came in handy. The workpeople's expertise at improvisation meant they could turn out prototypes of new weapons with surprising speed. By 1945 Jowetts had doubled in size and was all set to produce its most famous car, the Jowett Javelin, a 13 h.p. car which would do 80 m.p.h. yet consistently won tests. It came out in 1947 and was followed by the sports car, the Jowett Jupiter, which won the 1½ litre class in Monte Carlo rally. But the success was short-lived. In 1954 Jowetts sold out to the tractor manufacturers International Harvesters.

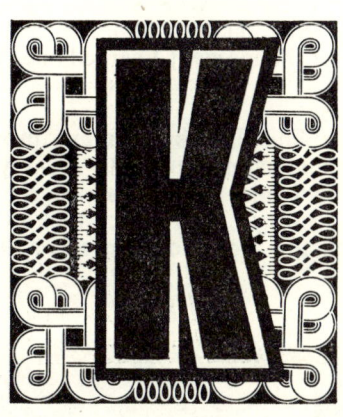

CHERRY KEARTON : The pioneer of all those nature films, Cherry Kearton was born at the village of Thwaite, the son of a Swaledale shepherd who was himself noted for his lantern lectures on birds. At the age of 13 he left for London to join his crippled brother Richard who wrote natural history stories. Deciding to illustrate the tales, Cherry bought a second-hand camera for 14s and took his first picture — of a thrush's nest on a friend's Yorkshire farm. It was the beginning of a partnership which produced 30 illustrated natural history books. A great traveller, he spent 35 years in South and East Africa, often risking his life to obtain shots of the animals in their natural surroundings. Once he was encircled by 16 lions. One sprang at him but he killed it with his last cartridge. He had another narrow escape in 1908 when he took the first cinema film from the air, clinging to three bamboo poles in the gondola of the Spencer brothers airship. The airship crashed outside London but Kearton escaped unhurt.

KILBURN : Throughout his life Yorkshire's master woodcarver Robert Thompson, "the Mouse Man," was associated with the White Horse of Kilburn. The horse, 314ft. long by 228ft. high, was conceived in imitation of the Berkshire white horse by Thomas Taylor, a native of Kilburn, who made his fortune in London out of the sale of York hams. It was designed by local schoolmaster John Hodgson and it took 31 villagers a month to cut it in the hillside in 1857. Apart from wartime when it was covered with turf and netting, Mr. Thompson looked after the White Horse for more than 30 years until his death in 1955, whitening it with disused carbide. A craftsman in oak, whose church furniture can be found in Westminster Abbey, York Minster and 700 churches throughout the country, Robert Thompson's hallmarks are an undulating surface produced by an adze, and the famous mouse which he carved on all his work. Describing how he chose the trade mark, he said "I was carving a beam on a church roof when another carver murmered something about us being as poor as church mice, and on the spur of the moment I carved one."

KILNSEY CRAG : This Dale's landmark provides three separate challenges to the fit and courageous. At Kilnsey Show (held in the shadow of the crag by Upper Wharfedale Agricultural Society since the beginning of the century), fell-runners race up and down the crag in an attempt to crack the record of 8 minutes 19 seconds. The over-

Kilnsey Crag as seen from the main Wharfedale road

(D. Binns)

30

hang itself is a stern test for rock-climbers and it remained unclimbed until 1957 when it was conquered in 11 hours by R. Moseley and J. Sumner from Manchester. Lesser mortals attempt to hit the rock face with stones thrown from the road. It looks easy enough though few have done it. Among them is former Yorkshire captain Brian Close.

LEEDS AND LIVERPOOL CANAL: Of growing popularity to leisure cruisers who don't mind the 4 m.p.h. speed limit or the 91 locks and 300 bridges throughout its 127 mile length. Partially constructed by engineer John Longbotham, the first section, from Bingley to Skipton was opened on April 7, 1773, though the entire canal was not completed until 1816. The total cost was £1,200,000. At one time in the early 19th century over two million tons of freight was carried. Now there is just the odd barge carrying coal or heavy cargo. **(See photograph on page 18.)**

LIFEBOATS: On the flat, narrow, windswept spit of land at Spurn Point at the tip of the Humber Estuary, live the families of the Royal National Lifeboat Institution's only full time crew. It is a lonely life, four miles from the nearest village of Kilnsea, and the lifeboatmen spend their time fishing, looking after a few sheep and chickens, or making models of the lifeboat or fancy bell ropes. One of the most dramatic and dangerous rescues was of the nine-man crew of the trawler *Gurth* in February 1940 during a long period of blizzards and bitter gales. "It was as black as your hat when we ran ashore," said the skipper of the *Gurth*. "We sent up rockets and I burned my bed as a flare". With visibility down to nil, *City of Bradford II* was launched in terrifying seas. Time and again the lifeboat vanished and rose again. Despite a fouled propeller, the lifeboat made a series of rushes and took off all the crew, groping her way back to Grimsby by searchlight. The coxswain received the George Medal and each member of the crew the Silver Medal. Equally hair-raising in a different way was the 1941 rescue of the crew of the *Thora* which was stuck in the middle of a floating acoustic minefield at the mouth of the Humber. Bathed in the glare of searchlights the lifeboat picked her way through the mines on one muffled engine to take off the eight members of the *Thora's* crew, and edged back to safety.

LYKE WAKE: Eerie enough to send shivers up your spine, the strangely beautiful Lyke Wake Dirge has been sung by mourners in North Yorkshire for centuries, albeit at only the occasional funeral. The dirgers sang while keeping vigil on the corpse while the fire was kept burning in the grate. The soul is visualised as embarking on a journey through a kind of purgatory and only obtaining passages through the perils of Whinney Moor, t'Brigg of Dread and the flames of hellfire if the person has been charitable in life. The chorus is appropriately chilling:

> *This aye neet, this aye neet*
> *Ivvery neet an' awl*
> *Fire an' fleet an' candleleet*
> *An Christ tak up thi sowl.*

It was the morbid fascination of the Lyke Wake Dirge which helped to popularise the 40-mile long distance footpath route across the North Yorkshire moors, the now famous Lyke Wake Walk which has been tramped so many times since 1955 that it has worn a wide bare track along the uplands. The Lyke Wake Club has instituted a spurious hierarchy of walkers who have completed the route several times, including Master of Misery, Doctor of Dolefulness and Past Master with a coffin badge for those whose faltering feet complete the mileage in 24 hours. First person to complete 100 Lyke Wake Walks was Louis Kilscar, and the speed record is held by Philip Puckrin who clocked up a time of 5 hours in 1972.

JOHN METCALF: Better known as "Blind Jack of Knaresborough," was an extraordinarily successful roadbuilder who made many of the major Yorkshire and Lancashire highways, and an even more extraordinary man. Born the son of a Knaresborough labourer in 1717, he was blinded by smallpox at the age of six but it never proved a handicap. He learnt to swim (and rescued a body entangled in the River Nidd), went hunting, became an expert violinist, could assess weights by measuring them with his arms and, it was said, could "feel" the pips on a playing card. Not only did he march north with the King's Army in the Jacobite Rebellion of 1745, setting up business contacts en route, but he also eloped with a Harrogate lady on the eve of her marriage to another man. When he died at Spofforth in 1810 he was survived by 114 direct descendants.

METEORITE: A rare event — a near miss by a meteorite — is commemorated by an obelisk in a field at Wold Newton in East Yorkshire. It happened in 1795 and Mr. Edward Topham, who lived in the village, recorded that the meteorite fell within two fields of his house. "John Shipley, one of my farming men," he wrote, "was so near the spot where it fell that he was struck very forcibly by some of the mud and earth raised by the stone dashing into the earth, which it penetrated to the depth of twelve inches, and seven afterwards into the chalk rock, making in all a depth of 19 inches from the surface."

MINING IN THE DALES: There may be gold in them thar fells. J. C. Cutcliffe Hyne, the author of the "Captain Kettle" adventure stories, claimed to have found gold dust in the streams near his home at Kettlewell. But the fortune of the Yorkshire Dales was based on lead with a little help from barytes, fluorspar, zinc and a little silver. Now a fallen heap of stones, which were once a smelting mill or a gaping mine level, are all that remain of an industry which in the 18th century made Swaledale, Grassington Moor and Greenhow Hill busier places than the infant towns of Leeds and Bradford. It reached its peak in the mid-19th century when 14 mines produced 12,000 tons a year. It was said that the Duke of Devonshire's mines made up to £70,000 a year.

Lead was mined in Yorkshire long before the Romans came, and some lead pigs (blocks) bearing the names of Roman emperors dating back to 81 A.D. have been found at Greenhow Hill. You can still see some of the early bell pits, narrow vertical shafts which descended about 20ft., from which the loads of bourse (a mixture of rock, spar and ore) were hauled up in a bag or bucket. When the shafts collapsed they left a characteristic bell-shaped funnel. The old-time miners made their own "Laws and Customs" whose origins can be traced back to the Roman mines in Spain. The 33 customary laws governing the Yorkshire Dales were drawn up at Grassington on May 2, 1737, by a Grand Jury of "24 ancient and skilled miners" elected from all the mining communities in the area. A jury of miners was called twice a year on Court Days at Easter and Michaelmas to administer the laws and they could impose a fine for bad workmanship or neglect of a mine. The highest penalty, a £5 fine, was reserved for a miner found working another man's seam. If a miner discovered a new vein he was entitled to a grant of two meers of ground along the vein, which was the distance he could throw his "hack" or pick both ways of the vein. In Wharfedale the meer was declared to be 30 yards but in Littondale and Langstrothdale the miners appear to have been mighty throwers, because their measure was 32 yards.

Lead mining was always a tough life. The journey to work was likely to take an hour's hard walking over rough moorland. With them they carried their lunch, slabs of wheatcake and home-made cheese which they often toasted over a candle flame, soda cake and a tin of tea. Wearing clogs, moleskin jackets and tight-fitting trousers so that their clothes wouldn't snag on rocks, the miners ventured underground with candles hung from a big button on their jackets. At the face they would fix the candles to the wall with wads of clay while they got down to the arduous business of making a hole to take explosive by hammering a steel bar into the rock. If they were working near a smelt mill there was the danger that the powerful fumes, which turned the grass yellow, might come swirling into the "level" leaving miners feeling ill for the rest of the day. Their one pleasure was a smoke: thick black twist crammed into the bowl of a clay pipe.

The mid-19th century boom in lead mining was soon followed by its complete collapse. Major seams were worked out and cheap lead from Spain, America and Australia made Yorkshire mines uneconomic. One of the last successful mines was Cononley near Skipton, many miles from the main lead mining areas. In under a century it produced 15,000 tons of lead ore and up to 550 tons a year (in 1863). By 1882 it was almost abandoned. The Dales lead mines lie gaunt and deserted but it is said that T'Owd Man (the generic name for all dead lead miners) may still be heard. There are several sober tales of the clicking of ghostly clogs on the Greenhow Road, and one man swore he heard the sound of a bicycle and a be-clogged miner alighting, when nothing of flesh and blood was near. **(See photograph on page 20.)**

NAVVIES: Yorkshire's canals, railways and more recently the M62, the most windswept motorway in the country, were built by the pick and shovel boys, the navvies, originally from Cumberland, more latterly Ireland. Their true name is "navigators" and they have always been recognised as the cream of the labourers, hard-working, hard-drinking men with their own way of life. One of their most remarkable exploits was the building of the Settle-Carlisle Railway, completed in 1876. In the wild moorland at Ribblehead, where bogs swallowed up hundreds of tons of infill and the rain sometimes seemed that it would never stop, the navvies made their shanty towns, colourfully named after battles ancient and modern — Jericho, Sebastopol and the largest, Batty Green. It was a wild, unruly life they led with an estimated 312,000 gallons of ale and 250 gallons of whisky sold there in a single year, and wives "sold" for a gallon of beer. Their favourite sports were dog racing, cock fighting and bare-knuckle fighting in which the contestants battled until they fell exhausted, a vigorous, incorrigible group of men and women who attracted preachers, bent on their reform, and tommy shop operators bent on acquiring their hard-earned money.

NEW YEAR'S EVE : Although one of the most persistent customs, the simple tradition of First-Footing in the early minutes of New Year's

Day is slowly dying. In the last minutes of New Year's Eve a dark-haired man (the Sex Discrimination Act has no sway here) stands shivering in the porch carrying a lump of coal, a pinch of salt and a biscuit or some other eatable, waiting for the church bells to ring. As he crosses the threshold he wishes good luck and prosperity to the house and its inhabitants and is rewarded with a glass of wine or something stronger. In bygone times it was also the time when the family finished the last of the Christmas frumenty — that spicy delicacy which dates back to Elizabethan times and probably earlier.

New Year's Eve — First Footing at an inn on Blackstone Edge

NOVELISTS : Yorkshire is extraordinarily rich in its novelists, both living and dead, with the Brontes and J. B. Priestley at the apex. The county has developed almost a style of its own: the sympathetic family saga with roots which dig deep into local history. One of the best is Dr. Phyllis Bentley's *Inheritance* trilogy which harks back to the troubles of the Industrial Revolution. Dr. Bentley had problems of her own in her youth when her father, a woolman, trembled on the brink of bankruptcy. In the miseries of the Depression she wrote *Inheritance*. Published in 1932 it was an immediate success and was translated into 23 languages. The final accolade came six years ago when it was serialised on television.

Winifred Holtby's *South Riding* which was revived not long ago as a television serial is one of the great classics of Yorkshire literature. Yet when she wrote it she was suffering from a fatal kidney illness and as she wrote she was often in so much pain that she cried over the paper. Born at Rudston, near Bridlington, in 1898 she wove her native countryside and her relatives and friends into her book, which was inspired by her mother's experience as the first woman on the East Riding County Council. A friend of authoress Vera Brittain, she travelled widely and lectured on radical subjects. She died in 1935, six months before *South Riding* was published.

36

Robin Hood's Bay, a famous Yorkshire coast fishing village
(Geoffrey N. Wright)

Skipton Castle's Round Tower

(Clifford Robinson)

The Valley of Desolation, near Bolton Abbey

University architecture as seen in one of the new science buildings at Leeds University

A Worth Valley Railway train arrives at Oxenhope in wintry weather   (Clifford Robinson)

York Minster, with the market in progress in the foreground   (Jack Wetherby)

The Zoo at Flamingo Park, near Malton, numbers this polar bear among its one thousand animals, birds and reptiles

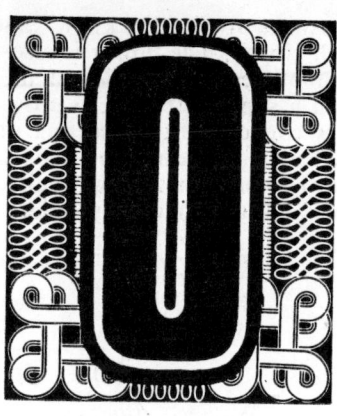

RICHARD OASTLER : His opponents labelled him ironically "The Factory King," but millworkers affectionately called him "King Richard" and went short themselves to bring him money and a few provisions when he was in Fleet Prison for debt. Richard Oastler, who fought for 20 bitter years for the Ten Hours Bill (passed in 1847), was one of the great Victorian reformers. Born in 1789, the son of a prosperous Leeds merchant, Richard Oastler had little taste for business and went bankrupt. It was in 1829 that Bradford woolman John Wood described to him conditions in the town's mills where ragged infants worked up to 18 hours a day and were beaten if they slacked. A considerable orator. Oastler fought the millowners with often vitriolic speeches and pamphlets. The struggle broke his health, though it was 1861 before he died. But he won.

ONIONS : Yorkshire folk have always had a taste for pickled onions and the family firm of Shaws, Wakefield Road, Huddersfield, has been catering for it off and on since the early years of the century. Most of their 300 tons of onions a year come from the Norfolk fields but during the summer they must rely on the high quality but high-price Egyptian varieties. That rankles, and strenuous efforts are being made to breed a summer British onion. In the early days the onions had to be topped and tailed and skinned by hand. Now sophisticated machines do the job. Although substantial quantities of pickled onions are exported to Southern California and to Boston on the East Coast of America, the bulk goes to the immediate Huddersfield-Bradford area. Pickled onion fans love the taste of the malt vinegar so much that Shaw's sales are soaring, though nationally pickled onions are slightly on the downgrade.

ORCHID : Yorkshire's rarest wild flower is the Lady's Slipper Orchid which still grows (it is believed) in a secret place in the Dales.

Only a handful of botanists are "in the know" and they make clandestine visits to ensure all is well. The flower is also known in Normandy where it is called "Sabot de la Vierge" and in fact its bloom looks more like a sabot than a slipper. It used to grow in Littondale, where certain country lovers concealed it by cutting off the flower when it appeared. All was well until an Edinburgh professor of botany offered a guinea for the root. The one remaining specimen was discovered by a villager and the blood (or sap) money paid.

The Lady's Slipper Orchid, a Yorkshire rarity

ORGANS : It is claimed that the organ at Leeds Town Hall is one of the finest in Europe. But the village of Cowthorpe near Wetherby might have had one of the strangest and most ornate. It was built by the talented, eccentric and almost unknown carver William Bellerby Harper in his thatched house. When the pipes became too large for the home, he cut holes in the ceiling and eventually transferred the entire organ to a barn. Nothing but the best was good enough for him.

He walked miles to save money on fares to buy exotic wood from abroad which he carved in a manner likened to the master carver Grinling Gibbons. His organ was to have 32 stops, two keyboards, a full range of pedals and 1,778 pipes. And he hoped the opening recital would bring him a wife. He should be glad, he said, "to have a large number of ladies and a very limited number of gentlemen" attending the recital. It is said he was offered several hundred pounds for the completed organ, but he died in 1917 before it was finished. The organ was sold in bits for £10 and the carvings were used to repair old farm carts.

OTLEY CHEVIN : In the 1800s zebras, wild hogs and deer wandered in the Danefield deer park on the famous Chevin to the north of Leeds. Nowadays it is the haunt of afternoon strollers. Its slopes provide one of the finest areas for bilberries and in late summer scores of people can be seen below Surprise View filling polythene bags with the single berries, dark purple with their white patina. Crowberries grow on the Chevin — they are blacker and more thickly clustered, but are too pippy to make good eating.

PENNY HEDGE : Every Ascension Day at 9 a.m., a peculiar hedge is built in the water on the east bank of the River Esk at Whitby. Known as the Horngarth or Penny Hedge, it has been built since the time of Henry II, and consists of three stakes, planted a yard from one another, cut with a knife (which once cost a penny) and capable of withstanding three tides. The story of the custom is that three barons, Percy, Bruce and Allatson, were out hunting a boar which took refuge in the cell of a hermit. The old man was at his devotions and refused to open the door to their cries. Enraged they

43

burst in and killed him. As he died, the hermit craved their forgiveness. So his murderers' lives were spared and they were allowed to keep their estates, which would normally have been forfeited. In return they made solemn promise that they and their heirs would perform the ceremony of the Penny Hedge. It is doubtful whether this is the true explanation and the reason for the penny hedge is a mystery which has exercised scholars for many years.

J. B. PRIESTLEY: Still writing with as much verve and pungency as ever, J. B. Priestley is a man of more parts than people realise. Beside being a sensitive landscape painter he wrote the lyrics for an opera, *The Olympians* in 1949, with music by Sir Arthur Bliss. And he once appeared on stage — in Bradford more than 50 years ago when he had a walk-on role in the opera *Romeo and Juliet.* "I wore tights with odd-coloured legs and held an eight-foot pike outside the church," he recalls. "I got half a crown for the one night — and passed it on to the man whose place I had taken." Born in Mannheim Road, Bradford, the son of a local headmaster, he was clearly destined to become a writer. When the family moved to Saltburn Place, Toller Lane, he scribbled away in an attic. His first article to appear in print was a regular feature for the *Bradford Pioneer,* the local Labour newspaper, while another early article was, strangely enough, on jazz dancing for a London magazine. He couldn't yet earn his living from his writing, so he took a job as a clerk in a Bradford wool office. It was a wonder, he thinks now, that he didn't get the sack. He used to dawdle on errands to the Conditioning House so that he could have a puff on his newly-acquired pipe, and looked forward to 7 p.m. when he could go home and start scribbling again. Although celebrated and sometimes criticised for his defence of old Bradford (his attitude was undoubtedly one of the reasons he had to wait so long before receiving the one and only honour he desired, the Freedom of Bradford), he also loves the Yorkshire Dales, which he considers the most beautiful scenery in the world, and when conifers were being planted in Langstrothdale he was in the forefront of the opposition.

JOSEPH PRIESTLEY: Using beer glasses, basins and a trough meant for washing household linen, Birstall-born Joseph Priestley who discovered oxygen 200 years ago, set about equipping his Wiltshire cottage as a laboratory for his revolutionary experiments into the nature of gases. The son of a Calvinist weaver and clothdresser (he was born in 1733) who worked at the looms in his cottage at Fieldhead, near Birstall, Priestley was brought up in the make-do-and-mend tradition. While at Leeds, where he was minister of the Mill Hill Chapel for six years from 1767, he made regular visits to the brewery next door — not to sample the beer but to watch fermentation.

He tested the degree of "bad air" on mice which he kept on a shelf over the kitchen fire. Apart from becoming one of our greatest scientists, he was a notable social philosopher. He believed that "government should interfere as little as possible with the lives, liberty or property of the members of the community," a sentiment which found its way directly into the American Declaration of Independence. While he and some friends celebrated the second anniversary of the Fall of the Bastille, a mob burnt his house, library and laboratory equipment, then said to be the best in Europe. Sickened of England, he emigrated to America in 1794 and died there ten years later — still an English citizen.

Joseph Priestley, the discoverer of oxygen

QUARMBY HALL, HUDDERSFIELD: Founded by Hugh de Quarmby who was slain in the so-called Elland Feud in 1340 by the henchmen of Sir John de Eland. His bloodstains, it is said, used to appear on a stone stair, though in fact the present hall dates from 1574 when it was built by John Blythe. Restored in 1945, part of the hall was divided into cottages and in one of these a living tree has been used as a beam.

QUARRY HILL FLATS, LEEDS: The flats are now destined to be demolished because of the high cost of repairs needed, but when they were built in 1936 for £600,000 they were the largest flats in Europe and regarded as "the greatest social experiment in England." Without the driving force of the Rev. Charles Jenkinson, Vicar of St. John and St. Barnabas, Holbeck, from 1927, they would never have been built. Moving north from Barking, he was appalled at Leeds' slums and made himself an expert on housing, drawing up statistics on overcrowding which were a damning indictment of Leeds housing. Elected to Leeds Council in 1930 on the platform "Clear The Slums" he became housing chairman and instituted great new re-housing schemes at Gipton, Moortown, Belle Isle and Seacroft. He disliked flats but it was the one way to re-house people swiftly. He determined that Quarry Hill flats, built on what had been one of the most squalid areas of Leeds, would have every modern amenity. Based on the Karl Marx House flats in Vienna they housed 938 families. For the time they were superb, but perhaps they were too big. Certainly the problems of achieving a true and harmonious community were never really overcome. **(See photograph on page 20.)**

QUILLERY: In the days of the great Yorkshire monastic houses, monks used to make their own paper, and careful of such expensive material they used the sliced-off edges of the paper to create artistic designs, an art which later became known as quillery from the quills used in the 17th and 18th centuries. As a hobby, Mrs. J. Robertshaw, of River Street, Haworth, continues this old craft, making scrolls and flowers from spare paper with the aid of a knitting needle instead of a quill.

QUOITS: Still played around Whitby and Robins Hood's Bay but has probably totally died out in other parts of Yorkshire. There was a proper 18 yards pitch at Meanwood Working Men's Club, Leeds, in the thirties and it was also played at Dewsbury. The real game of quoits is a very different business from the children's game with plastic rings. Quoits are made of iron, weighing up to 9 lb. and are heaved with strength and skill to fall (if the player is lucky) over an iron pin driven into the ground. Ringing the pin counts as two points, merely touching it as one, but you can also knock your opponents quoit away.

HARRY RAMSDEN'S, GUISELEY: Probably the best known fish and chip shop in the world. The shop which serves over 1¼ million people a year is the destination of scores of coach trips, and is even visited by American tourists based in London. The business was started by Mr. Harry Ramsden in 1928 when the first premises were a small wooden hut. The fame of his fish and chips spread rapidly so that by 1952 when Mr. Ramsden sold fish and chips at ½d a bag to celebrate the anniversary of the opening a crowd of 10,000 converged on the shop. It is now owned by Seafarers Restaurant Ltd. and has been given a £40,000 new facade and rebuilt kitchens. Despite the modernisation its popularity shows no sign of waning. On average each year it gets through 400,000 lbs. of fish and 400 tons of potatoes.

RHUBARB : In a wide crescent-shaped belt to the south of Leeds, stems of succulent rhubarb grow in profusion. Most is force-grown in the dark under low sheds, but rhubarb has even been found growing wild on the embankments of the M62. Rhubarb was introduced from Russia in 1578 as a botanical curiosity and at first people believed the acid-tasting stems were poisonous, despite the fact that it has been known as a purgative since Roman times. It took to Yorkshire like a native, probably because the soil, atmospheric conditions and some say the nature of the local sewage, used as a fertiliser, are just right. Now the Northern growers produce 75 per cent of Britain's 60,000 tons of rhubarb a year, most of which is sent for sale at Covent Garden and the other major London markets. Some is exported to France where the taste for rhubarb is growing. The varieties rejoice in such elegant names as Victoria and Albert, but in the trade rhubarb is known as bub, long strawberry or spring medicine. It has certainly earned the "medicine" tag. Valued for centuries as a laxative, it is said to be a remedy for acne and as a forestaller of the ravages of old age.

ROBIN HOOD : The outlaw famed in legend for his exploits in Sherwood Forest with his Merry Men was probably a Yorkshireman whose "stamping ground" was the forest of Barnsdale. Historian J. W. Walker identifies him as Robert Hood, born in Wakefield in 1290, who married Matilda (Maid Marion?) and was outlawed for taking part in a rebellion against Edward II. Many of the old ballads are set in Yorkshire including his battle with the "jolly pinder of Wakefield" who "leaned his back fast unto a thorn and his foot against a stone and there he fought a long summer's day, a summer's day so long." And, of course, it was at Kirklees Priory, near present-day Brighouse, where he died, betrayed by the false Prioress who allowed him to bleed to death. One of the most amusing of the Robin Hood ballads tells of the time when he found life too hot in the forest and tried his hand at fishing off the Scarborough coast under the name of Simon over the Lee. It turned out he was no fisherman:

> *They plucked up anchor and away did sayle,*
> *More of a day than two or three.*
> *When others cast in their bated hooks,*
> *The bare line into the sea cast he.*
> *"It will be long," said the master then,*
> *"Ere this great lubber do thrive on the sea.*
> *I'll assure you he shall have no part of our fish.*
> *For in truth he is no part worthy."*
> *"O woe is me!" said Simon then, "This day that ever*
> *   I came here;*
> *I wish I were in Plompton Parke in chasing of the*
> *   fallow deere."*

But Robin redeemed himself when the boat was attacked by a French man-of-war. He slew the entire crew with his longbow and towed the ship, filled with treasure, into port.

ROBIN HOOD'S BAY: A similar tale is also set in Robin Hood's Bay, the quaint East Coast town. The fishermen there had the reputation for brusqueness, even roughness to strangers but it was also known that they would brave the most treacherous seas to help ships in distress. Over the years the pounding waves have eaten away the cliffside and many houses have literally fallen into the sea. With half the village in peril, a new sea wall has now been built to buttress the northern cliff. **(See photograph on page 37.)**

ROYAL OAK DAY: Once celebrated in Yorkshire on May 29, it could turn out to be quite unpleasant. The custom was for everyone to carry a twig of oak, and those who failed to do so were likely to suffer the penalty of having their hands brushed with a nettle. The oak-leaf-less youngsters suffered an even worse fate, being rubbed all over with chalk — as well as being nettled.

SIR TITUS SALT: Now that Saltaire has been newly cleaned, it enables us to realise just how magnificent this "model village" must have appeared to the 850 families who lived there in the days of its founder, the Victorian millionaire, Sir Titus Salt, one time Mayor and later M.P. for Bradford. Although paternalistic and sometimes intolerant (he would cut down washing lines hung between the houses and refused to allow a public house in Saltaire), Sir Titus had the vision to build a total community round his "Palace of Industry," the alpaca wool mill, opened in 1853 with an immense banquet for 2,500 workers and 650 guests. While the dining room, where you could buy a plate of meat for 2d, catered for his workers' stomachs, his Congregational church provided for their spiritual needs and his social centre and library for their intellectual requirements. There they could study natural history, taxidermy and build steam engines or organs, and Saltaire's choirs and bands were famous throughout the district.

Born into a staunch Nonconformist family at the Old Manor House, Morley, Titus learnt woolstapling at Wakefield and proved himself a born businessman. His courage was tested at the age of 23 when striking woolcombers attacked a Bradford mill. Titus Salt went into the crowd and reasoned with them. Eventually the military had to be called out to quell the riot. After building his fortune on the little-considered Russian Donskoi wool and later on the intractable alpaca, he tended his business with precision. He was always at his mill before his work-people, was said "to make a thousand pounds before other people are out of bed" and his evening meals had to be served on the dot. A generous benefactor, his term as Mayor was marred by unemployment and five months of cholera. Salt opened soup kitchens, engaged 100 unemployed woolcombers, though he had no need of them, and visited the sick.

SHEEP: Unknown in this country, it is believed, until about 2000 B.C. Now they are almost a part of the landscape. Hardiest Yorkshire sheep of all are the Swaledales which flourish on the peaty ground in the upland area whose focal point is Tan Hill. On the Yorkshire-Lancashire border around Halifax you will find the long-eared lonk sheep, while Dalesbreds munch the grass in the limestone country of Craven. Shepherds still rely on black and white collie sheepdogs, thought to have been introduced by Scottish drovers, and if the air is quiet, the dogs can hear a whistle over one and a half miles. In the more remote parts of the Dales there are still some shepherds who use the extremely ancient method of sheep counting. In Wharfedale the numerals run: "yan, tan, tether, pathas, pimp, setha, letha, hava, dava, dik, yan-a-dik, tan-a-dik, tethra-dik, patha-dik, bomfit".

SHEFFIELD STEEL: At the heart of Sheffield's steel industry are the "little mesters," the craftsman-cutlers, many of whom employ less than five workers and have run the same firm for generations. The man who laid the foundation of good-quality steel was Doncaster clockmaker Benjamin Huntsman who was dissatisfied with the shear steel he was offered and opened his own works at Attercliffe. His secret of steelmaking was much sought after. It was said that one night Huntsman's workmen allowed a disreputable looking tramp to stay the night at the works. But the "tramp" turned out to be a rival manufacturer. His secret was out. Stainless steel was discovered in 1912 by a Sheffield man, Harry Brearley. Brought up in a back-to-back house he used to carry dinners to the steelworks as a boy. Rather than send his child to school, which he believed crushed an independent and original mind, he preferred to take a job in a new steelworks at Riga. Returning, he acquired the notion of manufacturing cutlery which would not rust, after making tests on erosion at a small-arms factory.

SKIPTON CASTLE : Above the impressive gatehouse of Skipton Castle stands the proud motto of the Cliffords "Desormais (Henceforth) which is particularly appropriate to the Elizabethan George de Clifford, the Third Earl of Cumberland who is credited with bringing back from his travels the shells and corals which decorate the remarkable Shell Room inside the gatehouse. Both on the tournament field, where he was Queen's Champion, and on the high seas, he sought adventure and nearly frittered away the family fortune in the process. During one of his nine expensive privateering voyages to the West Indies, he captured Puerto Rico from the Spanish but he lost half his 1,000 men through sickness and had to withdraw. **(See photograph on page 37.)**

STAITHES FEAST : The little fishing village of Staithes on the Yorkshire coast, where some of the older women still wear their lace caps, reminiscent of Breton fisherfolk, has always cherished its old traditions. And none was odder than the sports which they used to enjoy at the Staithes Feast in the 18th century. Man and wife had to run the course with the wife on her husband's back (no wheelbarrows allowed). In the skep and pole trial for married women the contestants had to balance on a pole, pivoting on a creel basket, and try to knock off a shell with a stick, a game which led to many upsets and laughter.

THREE PEAKS: The three highest peaks in the Dales, Ingleborough 2,373ft., Penyghent 2,273ft. and Whernside 2,414ft., have lured walkers, cyclists and runners to tackle all three in the shortest time possible. The record for runners is held by Jeff Norman from Altrincham, who took two hours 29 minutes 53 seconds to cover the 22 mile course which involves 5,000 feet of climbing. The cyclo-cross record, in which cyclists carry their bikes on their shoulders over the mountains, stands at two hours 37 minutes, 33 seconds by Eric Stone, of Otley, for a 25-mile course, set up in 1971.

TREES: Although not the original tree there is still an ash at the entrance to the village of Barkston Ash, near Tadcaster. Although now a small farming village, Barkston was once the centre of the Saxon Wapentake of Barkston Ash and it is said warriors and leaders gathered at the ancient ash tree to take major decisions. The Cowthorpe Oak, at the village near Wetherby, is reckoned to be 1,600 years old — the oldest oak in England. It looks it — all that is left is a section of the trunk, a ruin of a great tree.

FRED TRUEMAN: If ever there was an embodiment of the archetypal Yorkshireman it is the person of Fred Trueman, one of the great fast bowlers of the century. It wasn't simply his record which made the young lads on the boundary cheer themselves hoarse whenever he appeared on the field, though that is impressive enough: a world record of 307 wickets in Test cricket, a total of 2,301 wickets in first class cricket over 20 years, 67 Test match caps, 12 seasons in which he took more than 100 wickets, and a batting tally of about 9,000 runs. It was his personality which enlivened English cricket. He was cantankerous and controversial but full of heart and played the game to the hilt. From his first match with Yorkshire in 1949 he was a professional cricketer in every sense, with a driving will to win. Six foot tall with the stout legs of a paceman, he would give no quarter. The slightest hint of weakness from the batsman and he would come pounding up to the crease, his dark hair flapping and his arm whirling round like a vengeful broadsword as he flung down his terrifying bumpers. With the bat in hand he was equally dominant and often delighted the crowd with a superb six. His favourite position in the field was close-in where he had one of the "longest arms" in cricket. Yet he admitted to weeping in the dressing rooms after taking his 300th wicket in Test cricket against the Australians in 1964. While his dislike of authority endeared him to the crowd, his dry wit went down well with the players. Once when Peter May urged him on to greater efforts with the words "England expects . . ." Fred replied "That's why they call her the mother country!" Cricket lost a great character when he retired in 1968 at the age of 37 — unusually late for a paceman.

TYKES : The dictionary describes the Tyke as "an inferior mongrel dog or person with unpleasing, churlish and clumsy nature." Add a dash of wit and mischievousness and this is how Yorkshiremen are quite prepared for the rest of the country to see them. It is true that

A Tyke and his pleasures

Yorkshiremen adopted the nickname because of its sporting connotations. A tyke is the Yorkshire terrier used for hunting and poaching. And as Yorkshire is the county of sportsmen it came to mean anyone interested either as a spectator or participant in sport — especially in field sports, and perhaps the other kind as well. Joseph Wright, the remarkable Bradford "half-timer" who became our greatest authority on dialect, in his **English Dialect Dictionary** explains the term in this revealing quotation: "He is a tyke; he's allus toathree o' women i' t'wik. Shoo is a tyke: shoo's allus a toathree o' men at her heels". Hundreds of pot mugs, ashtrays and other cheap souvenirs show the Yorkshire Tyke revelling in his less charming role as a selfish skinflint. His toast is "Here's to me and my wife's husband, not forgetting missen", and his creed "Hear all, see all, say nowt, at all, sup all, pay nowt, and if ivver tha does owt for nowt allus do it for thissen". If nothing else a Yorkshire tyke is honest, as in a postcard from the early years of the century which bears the Yorkshireman's "Coat of Arms" and the verse:

Here's tiv us, all on us, may we niver want nowt, noon on us,
*   Nor me nawther.*
A Magny behold, a fly and a flea,
And a Yorkshireman's qualifications you'll see,
To backbite and spunge, and to chatter amain,
Or anything else Sir, by which he can gain.
The Horse shews they Buy few tho' many they steal,
Unhang'd their worth naught does the Gammon reveal
But let Censure stand by and not Bias the Mind,
For others, as bad as the Yorkshire you'll find.

U.F.O.s : Since 1947 when a Barnsley policeman reported a greyish white disc travelling fairly swiftly across the sky, Yorkshire has had its fair share of Unidentified Flying Objects. Few have been sensational sightings and no one has claimed to see little green men: what is significant is the similarity of the reports which have usually come from ordinary people who have been highly surprised to peer out of their bedroom windows at night and see a reddish-blue object with a tail which broke up over an hour (Guiseley, 1964) or a circle of lights like a fairground roundabout which passed over to the sound of muffled booms (Bradford, 1971). Of the many sightings one of the most unusual was that of a Batley man in 1968 who claims to have almost driven beneath a flying saucer which hung over the road at night. "I stopped and got out for a closer look. There seemed to be a lot of red lights hanging over the road in a rough diamond shape. The others were what seemed to be a row of portholes." It is hardly to be wondered that U.F.O.-enthusiasts have been active in Yorkshire, or that the first Northern Convention of Contact (U.K.) — a flying saucer-watchers' association — should be held at Ilkley in 1967. Disappointingly no U.F.O.s put in an appearance.

UGGLEBARNBY : The little village near Sleights, and not far from the East Coast, bears one of the most outlandish names to be found in Yorkshire. It owes the distinction to the Norse raiders who landed at Scarborough, the town being burnt by Harald Hardrada. They settled inland giving harsh names to small farming villages like Ugthorp, Fylingthorpe and Sigglesthorpe.

UNDERCLIFF : The area punctuated by green pools and boulders beneath Yorkshire's highest cliffs which rise 600ft. to Ravenscar. The Undercliff can only be reached with some difficulty on steep zigzagging footpaths, but despite this difficulty there was once high hopes of creating at Ravenscar (once known as The Peak) a popular seaside resort. Money ran out and nothing became of the idea. All there is at Ravenscar today is an hotel, a small golf course and some roads along which houses were never built. A sad place.

UNIVERSITIES : First student to enrol in 1874 at the Yorkshire College of Science, forerunner of the 70-year-old Leeds University, was a bearded miner called Shadrach Stephenson who brought his own paper with him and for two days had the sole attention of three professors. The University, whose Chancellor is the Duchess of Kent, received a munificent gift of £200,000 in 1936 from Frank Parkinson, "England's shyest millionaire."

Although its origins stretch back to the Bradford Technical College, founded in 1882, it wasn't until 1965 that the College of Advanced Technology was upgraded to become Bradford University, which was opened by the Chancellor Mr. Harold Wilson, then newly elected Prime Minister. With increasing numbers of students the Yorkshire universities keep on growing. The new buildings are all in the modern vein — but in very different styles. **(See photograph on page 39.)**

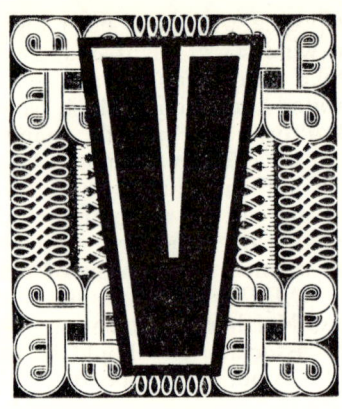

VALENTINE: A triple Valentine greeting was sent in 1840 to the three Bronte sisters by the Rev. William Weightman, who was then curate to the Rev. Patrick Bronte at Haworth. Charlotte, who was then 24, replied in cheerful vein:

A Roland for your Oliver
We think you've justly earned,
You've sent us each a Valentine
Your gift is now returned.
We cannot wink or talk like you;
We're plain folks every one.
You've played a clever jest on us;
We thank you for your fun.
Believe us when we frankly say
(Our words, though blunt, are true)
At home, abroad, by night or day
We all wish well to you.

Their good wishes brought poor Weightman little luck. He died aged 28 and is buried in Haworth churchyard.

VALLEY OF DESOLATION: Situated near Bolton Abbey, one of Yorkshire's most beautiful places, the valley reputedly owes its unusual name to a violent thunderstorm in the 18th century which killed many trees, leaving skeleton trunks of blasted oaks and grotesque and contorted thorns. **(See photograph on page 38.)**

VICUNA: Imports of the world's most expensive wool — from the rare vicuna, the South American llama, have been banned since 1970. Until then several West Yorkshire mills used to make vicuna cloth, priced at £65 a yard! It took the fleeces of 40 vicunas to make one average sized coat and at one time vicuna coats were so popular that the ever-opportunist Yorkshire textile men developed imitation vicuna made from shoddy.

VIKINGS: The spiky, guttural place names of the East Coast and the higher Dales like Ravenscar, Gunnerside and Arkengarthdale owe their origins to the Vikings who came to the North in the early tenth century, not from Scandinavia, but from Ireland. For many years there was trade and traffic between York and Dublin, but most of the Norsemen kept to the bleak unwanted uplands in Cleveland and Swaledale where they established scattered settlements at the dale heads. Evidence of the kind of life they led is contained in the names they left behind. As Arthur Raistrick, the celebrated geologist and historian from Linton points out, Winterscales and Summerscales refer to scale — the temporary hut or shed used by cowherds and shepherds, while gris (a pig) occurs in Grizedale. Some place names are survivals of the names of farmers or chieftains. Yockenthwaite comes from Eogan's thwaite — the clearing belongs to an Irishman, while Scarborough comes from Skarthi's burgh or town.

WAFFLES: Although once made in country kitchens, waffles could only be obtained commercially from Scarborough where they were—and are—sold at one shop on the promenade not far from Peasholm Park. The original waffle is a flat unsweetened biscuit made from a kind of batter mixture topped with jam and lashings of cream. Now they are sold in all flavours, sweet and savoury — but enjoyed just as much.

WAINHOUSE TOWER: Rising 253 feet high above Halifax, it was built as a chimney in 1871 by John Wainhouse to reduce the smoke nuisance from his dyeworks. When Wainhouse sold his mill,

the new owner did not take kindly to spending money on the underground passage to take the smoke to the chimney, so Wainhouse,
who loved beautiful things, had it converted into an ornamental tower,
with a lookout platform reached by 400 steps. It seems there may
have been a grudge involved, too, for the tower overlooked the garden
of Sir Henry Edwards at Pye Nest Estate, and destroyed his much-
cherished privacy.

WASSAILING : No old-fashioned Christmas in the Yorkshire
villages was complete without the wassailers who went from door to
door with their "wassail bob" made of rosemary, hoping to be invited
in for a slice of Christmas loaf, some cheese and a few coppers.

WEDDINGS : Old bridal customs continued in the Cleveland area
until recent times. Even now they pop up again on odd occasions.
Several vicars in the area made a stand against the paying of bride
money when the bridal procession is refused permission to leave the
church gate without casting a few coins on the ground. Young beaux
used also to race from the church to the bride's home for the honour
of claiming — and removing — the bride's garter, which was held to
give him luck in his love life. It was a custom which the more puri-
tanical members of the clergy were not sorry to see disappear.

SIR HAROLD WILSON : As Prime Minister Harold Wilson made
several official visits to his birthplace of Milnsbridge, Huddersfield,
where he enjoyed chatting with his old school and chapel friends. It
was from the pulpit of Milnsbridge Baptist Church, where he is
remembered as a chubby-faced Wolf Cub, a Sunday School scholar
and a call-boy for the church operettas, that he made his first public
address — as a 12-year-old at a Scout service. When about the same
age he earned his first money — by winning a prize in an essay com-
petition run by the Leeds Civic Society. The subject was "My Hero,"
and — as befits a keen Boy Scout — he chose Lord Baden Powell. He
has often referred with affection to his first school, New Street Council
School at Milnsbridge, where many of the children wore clogs but
received "the very best schooling." A scholarship took him to Wirral
Grammar School and Jesus College, Oxford, where he won firsts in
politics, philosophy and economics and became an economics don.
The way was open for an unparalleled political career.

WORTH VALLEY RAILWAY : Taking a fearful, though well
calculated risk, the Worth Valley Railway Preservation Society took
the plunge and started negotiations in 1962 to buy the closed Oxenhope to Keighley line from British Rail. Its boldness has paved the

way for other volunteer railway ventures at Embsay and on the North York Moors. For eight years now, steam locomotives have been chugging up and down the Worth Valley line. Except for the manager of the Oxenhope station shop the railway is operated entirely by amateurs and offers the public a chance to see some 35 steam locomotives and several diesels at the largest private railway museum in the county. There are strong indications that the railway has increased the popularity of Haworth itself, and it has certainly become known throughout the country because of its attraction to film-makers. It has been seen in more than 30 films of various kinds, ranging from the *Railway Children* to a wallpaper advert. The Keighley and Worth Valley Railway itself — (known locally as t'Grand Trunk) — was opened in 1867 after considerable delays caused by legal problems and a storm which washed away some of the embankments. The original estimate was £36,000, but in fact the railway cost nearly £105,000. Once built, however, it was highly successful, especially the freight side, which carried stone, slate, worsted and coal. **(See photograph on page 39.)**

YORK MINSTER : The £2 million task of underpinning the shaky 500-year old York Minster was one of the most remarkable of all ecclesiastical engineering projects. The discovery that the Minster had settled 13 inches on its rather jerry-built Norman foundations, and that the 16,000 tons central pillar was leaning out of true, was received with alarm. If nothing was done one of Britain's great treasures would collapse. While services continued in the Minster, engineers excavated the bedrock and filled the gap with a system of hydraulics set in a concrete raft. If the foundations shift again the Minster will move as an entirety. Stainless steel rods were inserted in the superstructure to prevent further movement and the huge 55ft. timbers in the roof which were found to be riddled with death-watch beetle were removed and replaced with concrete. To add the finishing touches the entire Minster was cleaned, mainly by scrubbing the ancient stonework with soap and water. When the job was finished in 1972 in time for the 500th anniversary celebrations, the Minster had acquired, in its hollowed out foundations, a new museum, the Undercroft, which now contains many of the Minster's treasures, some of which were revealed during excavations. It is now established as one of the North's premier tourist attractions. **(See photograph on page 40.)**

YORKSHIRE: We reach the heart of this book, Yorkshire itself, the county of broad acres. It has long been believed that Yorkshire contained 3,890,990 acres — more than the number of letters in the Bible. But four years ago a check revealed that the figure should really stand at 3,906,940 acres. Sadly local government reorganisation has made the figure irrelevant. On the fateful day, April 1st, 1974, Yorkshire was dismembered and its famous Ridings (or thirdings) cast aside in favour of five new counties. North Yorkshire, with 3,208 square miles, keeps alive Yorkshire's proud position as the largest county in England and the new West Yorkshire county boasts the fourth largest population in England with 2,064,000.

To Yorkshiremen their county has been far more than a line drawn on a map. Will the old feeling survive partition? South Yorkshire is clearly well within the fold, but what of Humberside (oddly similar in area to Winifred Holtby's fictional South Riding) and Teesside, neither of which carry the name of Yorkshire? So far there is every sign the Yorkshire spirit will survive the worst the Whitehall mandarins have done. We have however lost our two highest mountains, Mickle Fell, 2,591 feet high, has been swallowed by County Durham while the summit of 2,414ft. high Whernside (though not the main mass of the mountain) is claimed by Cumbria. On the other hand there have been large gains in the flat land south of the Humber at the expense of Lincolnshire.

YORKSHIRE PUDDING: A simple enough dish but to get it just right is the test of a good cook, and many a newly-married housewife has wept over her soggy lumps of batter, blackened round the edges. To be acceptable to the Yorkshire gourmet the puddings must be flat, light and crispy. Farmers' wives often used water and skimmed milk to make the batter — the important factor is that there should be no fat in the mixture. Traditionally it is eaten before the main course with gravy from the joint of beef, although old recipe books recommend cooking the puddings underneath the meat as it turns on a spit, so they soak up all the juices. Some people enjoy their Yorkshire puddings as a sweet with syrup, jam or sugar.

YULETIDE : In these days of smokeless fuel the custom is almost dead, but in the old days few households failed to bring home a yule (or feast) log on Christmas Eve, which had to be lit from the charred remains of last year's log. In the large Yorkshire country houses the servants took good care to choose a green, slow burning log because they would receive ale and cider with their meals as long as the log was alight. In the glow of the log would be eaten frumenty, the spicy delicacy made from wheat, and yule cakes, flat, thick discs packed with lemon peel, nutmeg, raisins and currants and topped off with a pastry network. Cottagers would enjoy bread and cheese marked with the sign of the cross. A welcome entertainment in rural Yorkshire was the visit of the Mummers, an eight-strong party who kept alive the ancient vegetation rites of death and resurrection. Until the 18th century, Halifax chandlers and grocers gave their regular customers Christmas candles which children kept burning in their bedrooms on Christmas Eve — presumably to see Santa Claus coming. And in Craven, Sunday school children received a traditional gift of buns on Christmas morning.

ZEPPELIN : The first Yorkshire town to be bombed by the German Zeppelin was the unlikely target of Driffield on June 14, 1915. The following day terror came to Hull when the Zeppelin L9 dropped 13 high explosive and 39 incendiary bombs, killing 19 people and injuring 40. Another five were reported to have died from shock following the attack. The great airship was fired on by batteries at Immingham and Waltham in Lincolnshire but escaped undamaged. Two months later the L9 struck again and this time it was Goole, which the Zeppelin captain mistook for Hull, that received a battering. In the raid 15 people died. After the first attack the Hull authorities took strict measures to black out the city and for much of the war it was known as the darkest city in England. No one questioned the necessity for these precautions. In all, the alarm sounded 53 times for Zeppelin attacks in which a total of 169 people were killed.

LORD ZETLAND: One of Yorkshire's great landowners — he owned 14,000 acres in the North East of the county — the second Marquess of Zetland lived dangerously. During his extensive travels in the East he narrowly escaped from an earthquake in Japan, an avalanche in the Himalayas and an attack by brigands in Arabia. But his closest shave was on the platform of Caxton Hall, London, where he was due to speak as Secretary of State for India and Burma. He was grazed by an assassin's bullet which killed Sir Michael O'Dwyer, Lieutenant-Governor of the Punjab. But the wound was slight and he lived on to the age of 84, dying in 1961.

ZOOS : With winds blowing clear across the Yorkshire Wolds, winter can be bitter cold at Flamingo Park, near Malton, one of the largest zoos in the country. Although the zoo remains open to the public all the year round, clocking up an attendance figure of approaching a million, winter doesn't worry the 1,000 animals, birds and reptiles. It is the combination of cold and wet which is the big threat, but the animals, most of whom are born in this country and thus acclimatised, grow extra-cosy winter coats and eat more food. Elephants and giraffes are particularly susceptible to the cold, and the chimpanzees are liable to catch chills, but turning up the heating solves most of their difficulties, and rarely are animals or birds lost through cold. "If we don't shut them up for the night we sometimes find the flamingos' feet are frozen into the ice on the pond," says Curator John Lang. "But they are hardy and rarely come to any harm. The other wild-fowl swim around and usually keep a small stretch of water free from ice. Marauding foxes pose a much greater problem — and people who take the waterfowl eggs."

In the 17 years since it began as a small menagerie, Flamingo Park Zoo has spread over 100 acres, employs 15 keepers, and takes in a total of 300 acres including a farm which produces mainly hay for the animals. The rest of the food is bought in bulk. Each week the creatures go through a ton and a half of hay, a ton of straw, four tons of grainstuffs, two to three hundredweights of birdseed, 1,000 lbs. of meat and over 16 stones of fish. Designed on the modern principle of keeping cages to a minimum and allowing the animals as much space as possible, Flamingo Park can claim their animals show every sign of being happy and contented. "They live longer in the zoo than in the wild, partly because they receive immediate medical attention. They don't have to hunt for their food and are quite happy as long as they have plenty of room," explains Mr. Lang. "The deer for instance

could easily jump out of their enclosure. They just don't want to."
Even so, there are occasional escapes. During one storm, wind snapped
the bough of a tree which fell into the racoons' enclosure. Three
racoons climbed the branch to freedom. One reached Bridlington
before he was caught — still in good health, probably because he had
fed from scraps nosed out of dust bins. **(See photograph on page 40.)**